Web Page Designer

Walter Oleksy

the rosen publishing group's
rosen central
new york

To Adam Anderson, a cool computer cat in Glenview, Ill., with thanks for his help on this book.

Published in 2000 by The Rosen Publishing Group, Inc.
29 East 21st Street, New York, NY 10010

First Edition

Library of Congress Cataloging-in-Publication Data

Oleksy, Walter G., 1930-
        Web page designer/ Walter Oleksy.
            p. cm.— (Coolcareers.com).
        Includes bibliographical references and index.
        ISBN 0-8239-3112-9
        1. Web sites—Design—Juvenile literature.
    I. Title II. Series.
        TK5105.888.0423   1999   99-55464

Manufactured in the United States of America

17.95

CONTENTS

ABOUT THIS BOOK

Technology is changing all the time. Just a few years ago, hardly anyone who wasn't a hardcore technogeek had heard of the Internet or the World Wide Web. Computers and modems were way slower and less powerful. If you said "dot com," no one would have any idea what you meant. Hard to imagine, isn't it?

It is also hard to imagine how much more change and growth is possible in the world of technology. People who work in the field are busy imagining, planning, and working toward the future, but even they can't be sure how computers and the Internet will look and function by the time you are ready to start your career. This book is intended to give you an idea of what is out there now so that you can think about what interests you and how to find out more about it.

One thing is clear: Computer-related occupations will continue to increase in number and variety. The demand for qualified workers in these extremely cool fields is increasing all the time. So if you want to get a head start on the competition, or if you just like to fool around with computers, read on!

chapter one

WHAT IS A WEB PAGE?

A fifteen-year-old high school junior in Evanston, Illinois, earned enough money working after school to put himself through college, and then some. Tim Dorsett did it by designing Web pages on his home computer.

In case you didn't know, a Web page is a site, or location, on the World Wide Web. The World Wide Web (or "www") is the name for computer files that can be reached through the Internet. The Internet

The internet is a system of computers connected by phone lines.

is a worldwide information network available through the use of a computer, a modem, an Internet provider, and a telephone.

What Tim did five years ago was so remarkable to most people that they thought it was magic or that he was a genius. It wasn't, and he wasn't. He just knew how to do something that was very new at the time, and people and companies were willing to pay him to do it.

Today Web page designers live and work in every city and almost every town. Tim's after-school business has turned into a career for thousands of people in the United States alone.

A Web page can be a person's own information page, telling others about his or her life. It can also be about something that person is interested in. For example, an eight-year-old boy in Minnesota made a Web page about a survey he conducted in his second-grade class about playing video games.

Web pages can be the sites of libraries, museums, universities, government agencies, or any organization or company dealing with or doing business with the public. These agencies may be in the United States or anywhere in the world.

A Web page can be one page on a computer monitor, or it can be many pages in what are called links. Links lead viewers to other pages of related information.

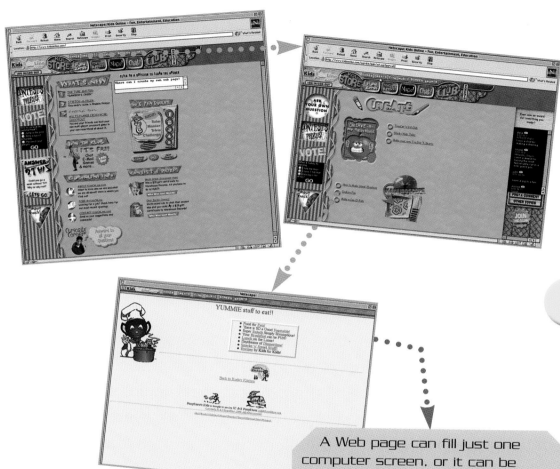

A Web page can fill just one computer screen, or it can be many pages linked together.

Someone with knowledge of how to design a Web page can find a lot of work. Some 44 percent of U.S. companies sell their products or services on-line, according to a 1999 report by the Association of National Advertisers. Another 36 percent reported that they were planning to do so in the next twelve months. Web site designers will be needed to

Businesses use Web pages to help them sell products and services.

8

create and maintain those new Web pages.

People who know how to create Web pages are in one of the newest but fastest growing careers in computer technology. The job of Web page designer didn't even exist about ten years ago. Only in the last five years or so has it grown into a career supporting tens of thousands of people.

Some people go into business for themselves as Web page designers. They design Web pages for other individuals who may just want a personal Web page about themselves or their special interests. They may also design Web pages for businesses.

Many other people work for Web page design companies. They may be writers, programmers, artists, or musicians who bring their own skills to the design of Web pages. They work either on staff or as consultants.

It is estimated that companies spend $19 billion a year on Web page design. Figures are not available on how many more millions of dollars individuals spend to have their personal Web pages designed.

This book will tell you more about Web page design. It will also introduce you to both young people and adults who either design Web pages for extra money or make it their career.

If you like working on a computer and learn how to design a Web page, you could choose a cool career as a Web page designer.

chapter two

WHAT WEB PAGE DESIGNERS DO

A Web page designer creates a page or site on the Internet for himself or herself, or for someone else. There were more than 12 million sites on the Internet in 1999. Thousands of new Web pages are added each day.

Web pages may be for individuals, businesses, institutions, or other public or private agencies. They may be used to inform, entertain, or sell a product—from paint to petunias. They may be Internet sites for the public to learn more about specific government agencies, cities, libraries, or a wide variety of other types of places or institutions.

Most Web pages contain both words (text) and illustrations (graphics). Illustrations may be photographs or artwork. They may be static; that is, they don't move. Or they may be movies.

Sound can also be added, such as spoken words or music. The artwork and sound can either be created by people or computer generated.

People in business for themselves may do everything in the creation of a Web page. They may

Web pages are often created by teams of people

be the writer, artist, musician, and programmer. Those who work for companies designing Web pages may have only one of those skills. They can become part of a team of people who create the Web page.

There are several job titles for a person who designs Web pages. Besides Web page designer, he or she may be called Web developer, Web producer, or Webmaster. Basically these titles all apply to people who do the same thing: create pages on the World Wide Web. A Webmaster may also oversee the work of a Web page designer.

THREE MAIN ELEMENTS OF A WEB PAGE ▶▶▶▶▶▶▶▶▶▶▶▶▶▶

The three basic elements of a Web page or site are writing, design, and programming.

Writing

The person who does the writing for a company's Web page may need to have special writing skills and knowledge of the company and its product or service.

For example, designing a Web page for a bank may require some knowledge of how banks operate. Designing a page for a scientific research firm may require a general knowledge of science or of a particular field of science such as electronics. If the Web page designer lacks the specific knowl- edge required by a company, he or she may work with a consultant to write the page.

The text for a

Web page must be easy to understand and grab people's attention. The style of writing will depend on what the owner of the Web page wants it to convey to the viewer. Writing for a rock music company's Web page may be in the latest pop-culture lingo. On the other hand, writing for a bank or insurance company's Web page will be less trendy and more formal.

Web pages always start with a "home page." A home page describes what the owner of the page wants viewers to know about it. It can be like the listing of a table of contents in a book. Or a home page can be more exciting. It can be text and/or illustrations that entice the viewer to learn more about the site.

Design

"Design" is a word for how the Web page looks. Since the text of a Web page may differ according to the nature of the owner of the page, its appearance also reflects the owner. A video game company's Web page may be full of excitement in the text and illustrations. A museum's Web page may be "quieter" and look more like the museum's traditional-looking brochure.

Web page design involves a blend of text, photos, and elements such as video and sound, if these are added.

Programming

Programming means putting instructions into a computer that tell it what to do. The instructions are written in any of several computer languages. In Web page design, programming is instruction given in computer language that tells the computer how a Web page is to be designed.

Web page designers should know the basics of all three skills—writing, design, and programming. They may not have to perform all three, but they should know enough about them to work with others who have those skills.

HOW TO CREATE A WEB PAGE ►►

First the content of a Web page must be written. It can be prepared and edited with any word processing or text editing program. Web pages are actually text files that are "tagged" with symbols to mark paragraphs, lists, headlines, quotations, and other structural parts of a document. The system of tags is called HTML (Hypertext Markup Language).

Although HTML may look confusing or complicated at first, it is not hard to learn. A shortcut to learning HTML is to use a template from Netscape, Microsoft Explorer, or another Internet browser. A template is an already prepared page. You just adapt it for the Web page you want to design.

The documents, graphics, video, sound, and other

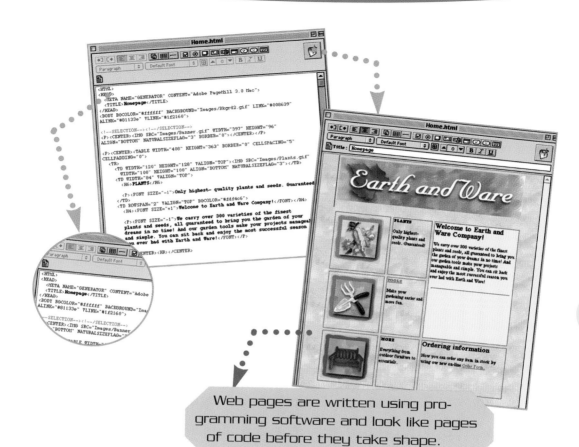

Web pages are written using programming software and look like pages of code before they take shape.

features of the page are then scanned into the computer. The Web page designer can make the site more exciting by writing scripts in Java, ActiveX, or other new Internet programming languages. This makes balls bounce, flags wave, or words move.

Multimedia capabilities for company Web pages allow designers to incorporate a wide range of audiovisual features into the sites. These may include use of a live audio feed from a radio station, music from tapes or CDs, or a live video from a press conference.

Web page designers often work with graphic artists to create unique graphics that distinguish the site from others on the Web.

There are more than 12 million Web

Web designers work with graphic artists to create unique, easy-to-use Web sites.

pages on the Internet, and thousands more are added every day. Each one of them was designed by someone, which means that a lot of people have found work as Web page designers.

chapter three

THE JOB OUTLOOK

Some people who design Web pages for individuals, companies, or institutions work as freelance designers. That means that they are self-employed. Others work for Web design companies that provide this specialized service. Still other people work for the company or institution for whom they design a Web site, such as an on-line mail-order company or a university.

Tens of thousands of companies and agencies have hired Web page designers over the past ten years. That is about when the new occupation of Web page designer began. Almost half of all of U.S. companies had Web sites for conducting business by 1999, and thousands more were planning to have Web sites for on-line business up and running by the year 2000.

Company spokespersons said that they had their Web sites designed with three objectives in mind: (1) to provide product and service information, (2) to increase brand and corporate awareness, and (3) to improve brand and corporate image (what the public thinks of the company and its product).

The average cost to develop a corporate Web site in 1999 was $252,000. The average cost of developing an e-commerce site was $369,000. An e-commerce Web site is a company's home page for conducting business with on-line customers. Companies spent about another $275,000 a year to keep their Web pages current and operating efficiently.

Major corporations such as IBM (International Business Machines) are especially in need of Web page designers. In 1999 IBM recruited more than 100 Web page designers. They were to become part of the company's

Large companies recruit qualified people with design talent to become Web page designers.

initiative to expand its presence on the World Wide Web.

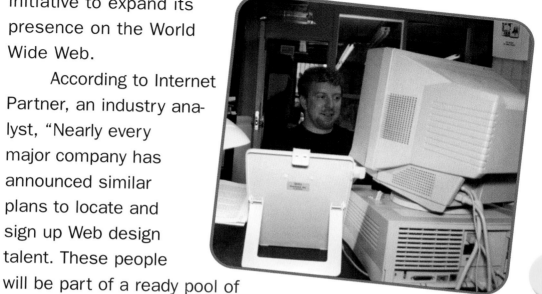

According to Internet Partner, an industry analyst, "Nearly every major company has announced similar plans to locate and sign up Web design talent. These people will be part of a ready pool of skilled technicians who can be called into play to design and launch solutions for corporations."

A spokesperson for one of the companies seeking Web design talent said that it is needed "so that we are able to solve any type of a client's problem using things from our bag of tricks. Web design is a major growth area that we are all going to find ourselves involved in over the years to come."

For the person with Web design skills, the salary is excellent, and the working conditions are often equally good. In California's Silicon Valley, where many leading computer companies are located, Web page designers and others with computer skills find themselves working in companies that look more like country clubs.

For example, Novell, in San Jose, California, is the world's fifth-largest maker of computer software. In 1999 the company opened its $130 million "work campus" with basketball, volleyball, and tennis courts; a gym; and a gourmet restaurant.

Thornton May, vice president for research and education at Cambridge Technology Partners,

Many of the companies that hire Web page designers have great facilities for their employees, such as basketball courts.

a consulting firm, explains why companies are so generous to Web page designers and other computer workers today:

"We are living in an economy that is driven by skills, and the skills bucket is close to empty. Companies are desperate for skilled workers. They'll do anything to recruit and keep you if you have the skills they need."

One of the most needed skills in computer technology today is Web page design, as more companies and institutions climb on the Internet site bandwagon. With all the perks, what career could be cooler?

A word of caution: the perks may be tempting, but Web page designers and others who work in the computer industry at high-tech companies really do work. The bene-fits are often provided because stressed-out employees need time out on the basketball court so that they can relax and recharge their batteries.

THE PAY IS GOOD TOO ▶▶▶▶▶▶▶

Salaries for Web page designers vary. If a person works as a freelancer, he or she will be paid by the job. Depending on how complex the page is, pay can range from a few hundred dollars to several thousand. Those who work for a company designing its Web page or for a firm that specializes in designing Web pages may earn $30,000 per year to start. A mid-level income can be nearly $50,000, and a top salary may reach $75,000.

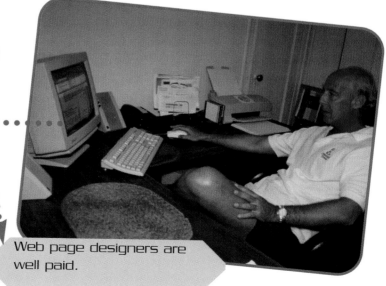

Web page designers are well paid.

The figures on what companies spend on their Internet sites mean that Web page designers earn good salaries creating them. Although it is expensive for the companies to have Web pages, the payoff is impressive. For example, in 1999 on-line Christmas shopping alone reached a record $3.5 billion. That accounted for nearly half of the total on-line sales for that year.

On-line sales from Web page businesses are expected to grow by almost thirteen times in the next few years, according to Forrester Research, a business research firm. It predicts that e-commerce sales will increase from about $7.8 billion in 1998 to $108 billion by the year 2003.

That means a lot of work for corporate Web page designers. With some $19 billion a year spent on business Web site development, page designers can often choose whether to work on staff or as consultants.

chapter four

TRAINING TO BE A WEB PAGE DESIGNER

Those who design Web pages need specialized computer skills, including both writing and programming skills. It is essential to have a knowledge of computer languages such as HTML and to know how to put graphics into a Web page.

Web page design terms and initials may sound like a foreign language. To most people, they are. To Web page designers, they are the tools of their trade, just as a carpenter's tools include a hammer and saw.

Says a spokesperson for International Data Corporation, "Because Internet programming technology continually makes it possible for Web sites to do more, developers can expect ongoing work. A degree doesn't matter as much as examples of creative work, training in Web

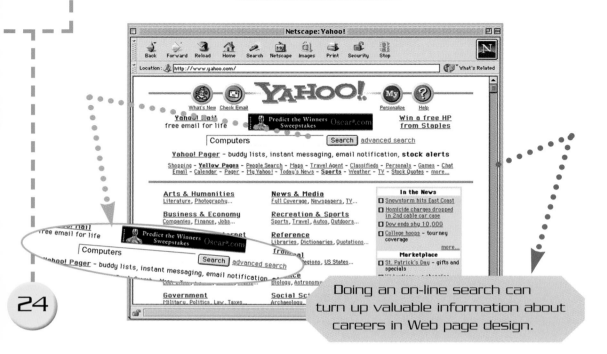

Doing an on-line search can turn up valuable information about careers in Web page design.

page design, and at least a year's experience working on a site."

If you do a simple on-line search for "Web page designer," you will access Internet sites about current job openings and what the requirements are.

WHAT COMPANIES WANT IN THEIR WEB PAGES ▶▶▶▶▶▶▶

Companies want many elements in their Web pages. One computer industry spokesperson says, "A company's Web site needs to fit its image. It has to give people a reason to keep coming back for more information or marketing hype. The job calls for knowledge of Internet programming language as well as old-fashioned creativity."

A Web page design firm in Los Angeles, California, posted a typical on-line sales pitch to potential customers who need a company Web site:

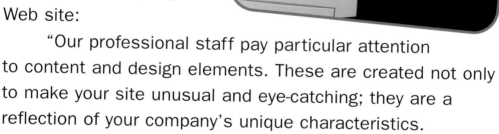

"Our professional staff pay particular attention to content and design elements. These are created not only to make your site unusual and eye-catching; they are a reflection of your company's unique characteristics.

"Whether designing a single-page site or multilevel interactive sites . . . whether you want sound, forms, tables, animation, image mapping, custom graphics, or something simple . . . we will bring your ideas to the world in an unforgettable and affordable way."

This gives someone thinking of working for the company as a Web page designer some idea of what is expected of him or her. There is also more:

"We believe in consistent and open communication with our clients," the firm's sales pitch continues. "We will never leave you dangling with unanswered questions or low-quality pages.

Job listings in newspapers and on-line will list the skills and qualities employers are looking for.

"It is this philosophy that over the years has earned us a reputation for leadership in creating Internet business pages."

The sales pitch concludes with, "Your Web site will be a visual representation of your business. It will portray the same image of professionalism that you would convey upon meeting a new client. For example, your Web site can include your marketing brochures or promotional information. This creates a consistent look between your virtual (Internet) business site and your actual local business site."

That may sound like a tall order for a Web page designer to fill, but it is generally what everyone wants from their Web site. To fill such a tall order, a Web page designer must have not only the specialized design and programming skills mentioned earlier. They must also have two other essential skills that cannot be learned but must come from within: imagination and creativity.

chapter five

PEOPLE WHO DESIGN WEB PAGES

We began this book about Web page design by telling about a boy who earned college money by designing Web pages while in high school. Tim Dorsett, now in college, explains how he did it: "I was fifteen and just cut from Evanston [Illinois] Township High School's sophomore basketball team. I was very disappointed but turned to my computer to get over it. I had always been interested in how some people became very successful going into business for themselves. I decided to try to become one myself, by creating Web pages for anyone who'd pay me to do it."

Tim worked after school and on Saturdays for a real estate company in odd jobs such as filing and running errands. He bought a scanner and used his parents' computer to start his Web design business.

"One of my first customers was Evanston's Chamber of Commerce," Tim recalls. "It hired me to create its first Web page. That led to me designing a Web page for the city's summer arts festival."

Tim designed a Web page for the *Evanston Clarion* that put everything in the weekly newspaper on-line. Publisher Tony Kelly said, "Tim put my paper on-line better and more complete than any other newspaper in the world at the time. He was just amazing!"

Tim's big break as a Web page designer came when he set up a booth at the Evanston Chamber of

You can get a start in a career as a Web page designer at an early age.

Commerce's technical exposition held in the city at Northwestern University in Evanston, Illinois.

"I looked like the kid I really was, until I put on a suit and tie and acted like I was a businessman just out of college," says Tim. "I sat at my computer and showed the businessmen Web pages of companies that were in competition with them. They hadn't even known about corporate Web pages or seen one before. They began asking if I could advertise their company by putting together a Web page for them. I said, 'Can do.'"

Tim was a can-do person at the age of five when he won a pizza-selling contest at school. At age twelve he earned $500 during the summer by running errands for senior citizen neighbors.

When potential clients at the expo learned that the tall young man at his computer was just a teenager, it didn't matter. An executive from Ameritech hired him on the spot to design a twenty-page Web site for the giant telephone and communications company in the Chicago area. That led to Tim, putting forty more clients on the World Wide Web over the next two years.

As college beckoned after high school graduation, Tim accepted a merger with a million-dollar computer consultant. Between what he earned designing Web pages and money from the merger, Dorsett is putting himself through college. His major isn't in computer technology, however; he wants his future to be in archaeology.

"It all began because I got bumped off the basketball team," Dorsett recalls. "Although it hurts when we are devastated by something, it often increases our desire and determination, and we become more motivated. We accomplish things that we never would have dreamed of previously."

ANOTHER YOUNG WEB PAGE DESIGNER ▶▶▶▶▶▶▶▶▶▶

Sue Kramer is a Web page designer and is only twelve years old. Although not yet a millionaire, Sue, who lives in a suburb of New York City, has also earned enough money to get a head start on college expenses.

Sue began working on computers early. When she was eight years old and in third grade, she won a design contest sponsored by a computer software company. She won a combination VCR and twenty-six-inch television set, $2,000 worth of movie tickets, a pair of sneakers, and lots of computer software.

"The first Web page I designed for money was two years ago," Sue recalls.

"It was for a neighborhood shoe store. The owner wanted to supplement his newspaper advertising by letting people with computers know about his seasonal sales. He learned that I designed Web pages by reading about me in the same local paper."

That led Sue to start her own Web design business, Webgirl. "I had heard about others by guys who called themselves Webmen," she explains. "I began with a partner, another seventh grader at my school, but she left and started her own Web design business. We're still friends, as long as we don't talk about our competing businesses."

BUSY AS A SPIDER
SPINNING HIS WEB ▶▶▶▶▶▶▶▶▶▶

Erik Meyer practically played on a computer in his crib. Today the new father-to-be designs Web pages and is hyper-media systems manager for Case Western Reserve University in Cleveland, Ohio.

"Before that, I was a member of the information technology departments of a university, a law publishing firm, and a pharmaceuticals company," says Meyer. "I've also been a radio announcer, an amateur actor, a drummer, and a burger flipper."

There's more: "I write fiction and computer programs,

cook, read, play the piano and violin, and have a bachelor's degree in history as well as minors in astronomy, English, and artificial intelligence. My hair is red, my eyes are blue, I'm still in my twenties, I got married last year, and I have to learn the nontechnical job of how to change diapers because I'll be a father any day now."

Meyer's first job at Case Western was to set up computers in the libraries and make sure that they kept working. When the first Web browser (Mosaic) came out, he saw how the World Wide Web worked and became fascinated by it.

"I learned how to create Web pages on my own time," says Meyer. "Then I encouraged my bosses to put the university on-line with a Web page of its own. They said that I was the natural person to run it, so that's how I got the job I have now."

Meyer may be busier than anyone else at the university. "In my campaign to have absolutely no free

Web page designers often have very busy schedules.

time whatsoever, I just had two computer articles published." He could write a book on how to design Web pages but offers this shorter version for advice:

"The basic part is taking words and fitting them into a structure that Web browsers can understand. To do that, you have to learn HTML, but it is pretty easy to learn.

"You also need to create pictures for pages—like photos of your dog or cool-looking buttons for people to click on. That's rather simple, too. In learning HTML, you learn how to add graphics to a Web page."

After that, Meyer says, you have some choices. "You can learn more advanced programming languages like Javascript, or other Web languages that can make your page look and act better."

There is one other thing a good Web page designer should do, says Meyer. "That's to arrange the information on the pages so that it's organized in a way that's easy to understand. It may be the most important thing a designer does. Good organization means a good Web site that people can use and come back to often."

Meyer offers this advice to future Web page designers: "Become familiar with computers. Knowing how to use your Nintendo isn't quite enough. Learn to use Windows or a Macintosh computer, and learn to use the Web design programs on them.

"Surf the Web. Go to as many sites as you can find. Notice how they look, how they work, and how they make you feel. Later on, the stuff you liked will come back in your own designs, which is fine.

"If you're artistic, that helps, but it isn't absolutely required. If you can write well, that's another big plus, as is the ability to organize things.

"The more varied your background is, the better Web page designer you'll make. I sometimes think that I'm a better designer because I have a degree in history than if I had gotten a degree in computer science. Do what interests you. You'll find it useful in Web page design.

"The best Web page designers understand computers really well, write clearly, and have some artistic talent."

If you want to see Meyer's Web site for Case Western Reserve University, go on-line to *http://www.cwru.edu.*

WORDS.COM: GLOSSARY

ActiveX   One of several computer programming languages used to design Web pages.

browser   Software applications used to surf the World Wide Web, such as Netscape, Java, and Microsoft Explorer.

data   Information that can be processed by a computer.

disk   A computer part used to read and record information.

e-commerce   Electronic commerce; business conducted on a computer and the World Wide Web.

e-mail   Messages sent electronically to and from different computers via a computer network.

freelance   A person who is self-employed.

graphics   Computer-generated art and illustrations.

home page   A person's or company's own site on the World Wide Web. Also the first page of any Web site.

HTML (Hypertext Markup Language)   Language used to write Web pages and create links that lead to more information.

hypertext   Data that link elements in a Web page.

integrator   Someone who combines text, graphics, and other elements of a Web page.

Internet   An information network available worldwide through the use of a computer, modem, and telephone.

Java   One of several computer languages used to design Web pages.

links   Connections between Web page documents.

modem   A computer accessory that translates data into tones sent over telephone lines, for sending and receiving text and graphics.

multimedia   The combination of sound, still and moving visuals, and text in one on-screen computer application.

network   A group of computers connected so they can all work together.

on-line   To be available on a computer information network.

program   The list of instructions that tell a computer how to complete a task.

provider   A company such as America Online that connects you with the Internet.

Silicon Valley   Term used for the area in California where many computer companies are located.

software   Computer programs that run the computer.

staff   A person who works at a company, as opposed to someone who works at home as a freelancer.

surfing   A term for browsing the Internet.

tags   Computer language symbols (like HTML) used in designing Web pages.

text   Words on a Web page.

Web   The World Wide Web or "www"; the name for computer files that can be reached through the Internet.

RESOURCES.COM: WEB SITES

Many sources are available in books and on the Internet to help you learn more about how to design a Web page. A good starting place to learn about Web page design is from a computer toy called Logiblocs. Like an electronic Lego building set, Logiblocs are various electronic "building blocks." They make it less complicated and even fun to learn many of the skills involved in programming and Web page design. Their Internet site is *http://www.logiblocs.com/educat.html*

An excellent free on-line information source on how to design a Web page is About.com. Jean Kaiser's Guide to Web Design at *http://www.webdesign.about.com* offers information on HTML, page layout, Web graphics, testing, and other elements of Internet page design. You can also meet Web page designers on-line at another of About.com's links, the Web Design Community Bulletin Board.

A Beginner's Guide to HTML is available free on-line from the National Center for Supercomputing Applications at *http://www.ncsa.uiuc.edu.*

Another source for learning about HTML is the HTML Writers Guild at *http://www.hwg.org.*

For a more advanced explanation of HTML and the structure of a Web page, visit Tom O'Haver's Web site at the University of Maryland at College Park: *www.wam.umd.edu /~toh/NetscapeHandout.html.* You learn about adding sound and graphics to Web pages.

LOOK UP SOME WEB PAGES▸▸▸▸▸▸▸▸▸▸▸▸▸▸

You can easily see how much some Web pages contain and how they differ if you visit a few of them on the Internet. You'll also see how text, graphics, and sound are used.

Surf the Web for these sites to see how different various Web pages can be:

- www.dabulls.com. The official Web site of the Chicago Bulls basketball team. At one link, you can see color photos of the team, including former star Michael Jordan. At another link, you can listen to audio files with the exciting closing moments of the team's championship games.
- www.worldkids.net. The Web page of World Kids Network. You access a home page that is a Site Overview page telling what links to go to. One link is to "Critters Area," which has information about prehistoric and extinct animals, endangered

species, bugs, and pets. Another link is to a chat room where you can communicate on-line with others who have similar interests.

💾 www.bluemountain.com. Blue Mountain Arts is a company that lets you send free animated and sound greeting cards for birthdays or holidays. The moving animation and bouncy music greeting cards are fun to watch, then e-mail to friends.

On-line Information

You can also get instruction in Web page design from various on-line sources, such as the following:

💾 www.microsoft.com/frontpage/. Microsoft's FrontPage Web site offers free on-line information on creating and managing personal or business Web pages. It has links to an on-line workshop and multimedia demonstration.

💾 www.businessnet.freeservers.com/. Netscape also has free Web site design information.

💾 www.cio. com/forums/careers/ . The Web Career Research Center offers free information on both Web page design and other Web careers.

Professional Web Page Design Sites

💾 www.iwanet.org/ . The International Webmasters Association has a wealth of Web design career information, in English, Spanish, and other languages.

www.thedaily.washington.edu/staff/martin/ resources.html. The Webmasters' Guild is a non-profit organization to educate, promote, and unify Web site developers worldwide.

Many public and private schools offer courses in Web page design. You can find them in the Yellow Pages of your local telephone book under Schools.

Another way to learn more about a career as a Web page designer is to meet one. If you look in the Yellow Pages of your telephone book or the classified ads in your local newspaper, you'll probably find at least one. If this person is not too busy, he or she may tell you what a career is like as a Web page designer. Then you can decide if this cool career is for you.

BOOKS.COM: FOR FURTHER READING

BOOKS ▸▸▸▸▸▸▸▸▸▸▸▸▸▸▸

Lund, Bill. *A Career as an Internet Designer.*
Mankato, MN:Capstone Press, 1998. Basic
book for preteens about working in Web page
design.

Eberts, Marjorie, and Margaret Gisler. *Careers for Computer Buffs.* Lincolnwood, IL: VGM Career
Horizons, 1999. A basic book on computer
careers, although nothing is included specifi-
cally on being a Web page designer.

ARTICLES ▸▸▸▸▸▸▸▸▸▸▸▸▸▸▸

Callahan, Steven, "Web Site on a Budget." *Internet
World*, April 1996, pp. 55–61.

Reichard, Kevin, "A Site of Your Own." *PC Magazine*,
October 10, 1995, pp. 227–238.

Richardson, Eric, "Site Construction." *Internet World*, April 1996, pp. 62–66.

Sigler, Douglas, "HTML Toolbox." *Internet World*, April 1996, pp. 51–52.

Snyder, Joel, "Good, Bad, and Ugly Pages." *Internet World*, April 1966, pp. 26–27.

ON-LINE▶▶▶▶▶▶▶▶▶▶▶▶▶▶▶

About.com: www.webdesign.about.com

Beginners Guide to HTML: www.ncsa.uiuc.edu

How to Make a Web Page:
www.wam.umd.edu/~toh/NetscapeHandout.html

HTML Writers Guild: www.hwg.org

Logiblocs: www.logiblocs.com

Microsoft Web Page Design: www.microsoft.com/frontpage

Netscape Web Page Design:
www.businessnet.freeservers.com

Web Career Research Center:
www.cio.com/forums/careers/

Webmasters Guild: www.thedaily.washington.edu/staff/martin/resources.html

INDEX

CREDITS

About the Author
Walter Oleksy, a freelance writer in Glenview, Illinois, has had over forty books published for young readers and adults. His other books for The Rosen Publishing Group include *CoolCareers.Com: Video Game Design* and *CoolCareers.Com: Web Entrepreneur*.

Acknowledgments
The author wishes to thank Tim Dorsett, a pioneer in Web page design, and the others quoted in this book for their generous computer career advice to young people.

Design and Layout: Annie O'Donnell

Consulting Editor: Amy Haugesag